Held Back But Not Defeated

Joshua Rhoades

Published by Joshua Paul Rhoades, 2024.

HELD BACK BUT NOT DEFEATED

First edition. November 8, 2024.

ISBN: 979-8227332387

Written by Joshua Rhoades.

Also by Joshua Rhoades

Courage Under Fire: David's Stand On The Battlefield
Jonah's Journey: Voices Of Redemption And Lessons In Obedience
The Furnace Of Faith: 12 Principles From The Heat Of Faith
Whispers of Hope: Inspiring Stories of Men's Prayers In Scripture
Frontier Legends: The Oregon Dream
Elijah: A Beacon Of Boldness
HOOK, LINE & SAVIOUR - Faith Reflections from Fishing
Driven By Faith: Motor Racing Inspired Christian Life
30 Day Devotional - Bold and Strong- Coffee Devotions for a Courageous Christian Walk
Authentic Christianity: The Heart of Old Time Religion
Consider The Ant - God's Tiny Preachers
Flee Fornication: The Plea For Purity
Renewed Hope- How to Find Encouragement in God
Sounding The Call - The Voice of Conviction
The Altar - Where Heaven Meets Earth
The Bible's Battlefields- Timeless Lessons from Ancient Wars
The Sacred Art of Silence - How Silence Speaks in Scripture
Under Fire- The Sanctity of the Traditional Biblical Home
Who Is on the Lord's Side? A Call to Righteousness
What Is Truth? - From Skepticism to Submission
First and Goal- Faith and Football Fundamentals
From Dugout to Devotion- Spiritual Lessons from Baseball
Par for the Course- Faith and Fairways
The Believer's Pace- Tools for Running Life's Marathon
The Immutable Fortress- Security in God's Unchanging Nature
Biblical Bravery
Deer Stands and Devotions: A Hunter's Walk with God

Jesus Knows- Our Hearts, Our Responsibility
Restoration - Setting The Bone
Spiritual 911- God's Word for Life's Emergency's
The Freedom of Forgiveness
The Jezebel Effect - Ancient Manipulations Modern Lessons
The Shout That Stopped The Saviour
The Time Machine Chronicles: Old Testament Characters
Anchored In Truth Exploring The Depths of Psalm 119
Biblical Counsel on Anger
Proverbs' Portraits The Men God Mentions
Stumbling in the Dark - The Dangers of Alcohol
Guarding the Wicket Protecting Your Faith and Game
The Champion's Faith - Wrestling and Achieving Spiritual Victory
Scriptural Commands for Modern Times Living God's Word Today Volume 1
Scriptural Commands for Modern Times Living God's Word Today Volume 2
Scriptural Commands for Modern Times Living God's Word TodayVolume3
The Greatest Gift
A Christmas Journey of Faith
Daughter Of The King: Embracing Your Identity In Christ
Determination and Dedication Building Strong Faith As A Young Man
Walking Through Walls God's Power to Part the Storms of Life
David's Song Of Deliverance Praising God Through Every Storm
From Weakness to Warrior: Gideon's Transformation
Why Did Jesus Weep?
Living For God The Call To Be A Living Sacrifice
My Mind Is In A Fog What Do I Do?
Turning The Page Written By Grace
The Calling and Greatness of John the Baptist
For Such a Time Esther's Courageous Stand
From Brokenness To Beauty Written By The Pen of Grace
The Ultimate Guide to Massive Action- From Plans to Reality
A Heart Of Conviction
Serving In The Shadows
Repentance Revealed The Road Back To God
The Chief Sinner Meets The Chief Saviour Reflections On I Timothy 1:15

Answer The Call - 31 Days of Biblical Action
The Birthmark of the Believer
Reflections on Calvary's Cross
The Kingdom Builder Paul's Bold Proclamation of Christ
The Animal Of Pride
The Reach That Restores Christ Love For The Broken
Paul- The Many Roles of a Servant of Christ
Unshakeable Faith- 31 Days of Peace in God's Word
O Come, Let Us Adore Him- A Christmas Devotional
The Shepherd's Voice
The Trail From Vision To Mission
Held Back But Not Defeated

Dedication

To you, dear reader, who has picked up this book not by chance but with purpose, this is for you. "Held Back, But Not Defeated" is more than a collection of words; it is a message of hope, resilience, and the unbreakable power of faith—written with you in mind. Life may feel like a constant series of trials. Maybe you know the feeling of facing one struggle after another, obstacles that seem designed to block your path, making every step feel heavy. Perhaps you've known discouragement, fear, or even doubt, wondering if you have the strength to keep going. If that resonates with you, you're not alone.

The journey of faith is often marked by unseen battles, and even the strongest can feel weary. But know this: within every hardship, there is an opportunity for strength and growth that only God can bring. Paul, the apostle whose life inspired this book, faced trials beyond what most of us can imagine—beatings, imprisonment, rejection, betrayals, and countless days of struggle. Yet, each setback, each "no," each closed door, didn't defeat him. His heart remained steadfast because he knew he was held in the hands of a faithful God. Like Paul, you have a purpose that no earthly obstacle can erase. You may be held back at times, but in God's grace, you are never defeated.

As you turn these pages, may you feel encouraged and uplifted. Know that the same God who walked with Paul through his darkest hours is with you now, offering strength, hope, and the courage to keep moving forward. This book is written for every heart that has felt weary, every soul that has felt blocked, and every person who has questioned if they could make it. Let Paul's story remind you that your trials are not the end of your story. Every challenge you face is an opportunity to lean into God's strength, to deepen your trust in Him, and to become a vessel of His enduring grace.

May you read these words and feel inspired to rise above every hindrance with a spirit that cannot be crushed. May you know that, in Christ, you have everything you need to press on. And may this book remind you that, while we may be held back at times, God has already won the victory.

"Wherefore we would have come unto you, even I Paul, once and again; but Satan hindered us." — I Thessalonians 2:18

This verse reflects not only Paul's relentless struggle but also his unbreakable resolve. Amid every barrier—opposition, imprisonment, betrayal—Paul's faith pushed him forward, undeterred. His life reminds us that obstacles are not defeat; they are moments to deepen our trust in God and to grow. May this book inspire you to press on, trusting that, though we may be held back, in God's purpose we are never defeated.

Introduction

In I Thessalonians 2:18, Paul writes, "Wherefore we would have come unto you, even I Paul, once and again; but Satan hindered us." This verse reflects the heart of Paul's struggle and his determination to continue despite intense opposition. Paul's life as an apostle was filled with obstacles that could have easily defeated someone less committed. He was frequently opposed by people who tried to stop his message, imprisoned for his beliefs, mocked, betrayed, and misunderstood. At times, it seemed as though every step he took forward was met with another barrier—yet Paul continued undeterred, driven by his love for Christ and his calling to spread the Gospel. In the face of these trials, Paul understood that his hindrances were not simply a series of unfortunate events; rather, they were spiritual battles, with Satan working actively to prevent him from fulfilling his purpose. Even when held back, Paul was never defeated, because he placed his confidence in God's power, not his own. This unwavering faith allowed him to press forward, using his letters to encourage and instruct the early churches even when he couldn't be physically present. His words, born out of hardship, became pillars of wisdom and strength for believers then and now. The book "Held Back, But Not Defeated" looks into Paul's remarkable resilience and examines how his experiences teach modern Christians to stand firm despite life's challenges. Today's believers may not face the same physical dangers as Paul, but they encounter their own battles—whether through discouragement, temptation, or situations that seem beyond their control. Paul's life is a reminder that obstacles do not signify defeat. Instead, they can deepen one's reliance on God, sharpen one's faith, and reveal God's strength in powerful ways. This book seeks to guide readers through Paul's story and highlight lessons that can be applied to today's struggles, showing that Christians, like Paul, can overcome obstacles with a faith that trusts God's timing and purpose. The message of Paul's life encourages Christians to stand firm, to view every trial as an opportunity for growth, and to trust that God's work will be accomplished, even in the face of setbacks. By exploring the strength Paul found in his faith, this book aims to inspire readers to embrace their own journey, confident that, while they may be held back at times, they can live with a spirit that is never defeated.

Chapter 1 - Strife

In I Thessalonians 2:18, Paul expresses a heartfelt desire to visit the Thessalonian believers, but he reveals that his plans were thwarted, saying, "Wherefore we would have come unto you, even I Paul, once and again; but Satan hindered us." This verse sheds light on a profound aspect of Paul's ministry: although he was one of the most dedicated apostles, known for his courage and resilience, he encountered persistent and powerful spiritual opposition from Satan himself, who tried to stop him from carrying out his mission. Paul's journey was full of challenges that could discourage anyone, yet he remained steadfast, relying on God's strength and pressing forward despite these roadblocks. One of the ways Satan sought to hinder Paul was by stirring up strife within the church, causing believers to turn against each other instead of uniting in their faith. In 1 Corinthians 1:11-13, Paul addresses this strife, saying, "For it hath been declared unto me of you, my brethren, by them which are of the house of Chloe, that there are contentions among you. Now this I say, that every one of you saith, I am of Paul; and I of Apollos; and I of Cephas; and I of Christ. Is Christ divided? was Paul crucified for you? or were ye baptized in the name of Paul?" Here, Paul points out the divisions in the church, as some believers claimed allegiance to different leaders like Apollos or Cephas instead of focusing solely on Christ. By doing this, Satan created confusion and division among the church members, distracting them from their true purpose and weakening their unity. Paul knew that such strife was dangerous because it could tear apart the early church and prevent it from growing strong in faith and numbers. Instead of allowing these divisions to persist, Paul took a firm stand, urging the believers to remember that Christ alone was crucified for them and that they were all baptized in His name, not in the name of any human leader. This message was essential for maintaining the church's unity and strength in the face of opposition. Paul's response to the strife in the Corinthian church demonstrates his deep understanding of how division can hinder spiritual growth and how unity in Christ is the foundation of a strong faith community. Despite Satan's attempts to create conflict and weaken the believers' commitment, Paul's teachings encouraged them to overcome their differences and focus on their shared purpose in Christ. Through this example, we see how Paul's resilience, wisdom, and unwavering focus on Christ allowed him to counteract Satan's schemes and guide the church back to unity. Although Paul faced many other challenges and obstacles throughout his ministry, his experience with strife in the church of Corinth serves as a powerful reminder of the importance of staying united in faith, even when confronted with forces that seek to divide and hinder us. Satan's attempts to create discord and division among believers did not succeed in stopping Paul, who remained devoted to his mission and continued to spread the gospel with courage and faith. This example of Paul's response to spiritual hindrance encourages us to remember that, although we may face opposition and challenges in our own faith journeys, we can overcome them by keeping our eyes fixed on Christ and standing united with our fellow believers. Paul's experience shows that even when Satan tries to hinder us, we can be "held back, but not defeated" if we trust in God's strength and remain steadfast in our faith.

Chapter 2 - Slander

In I Thessalonians 2:18, Paul expresses his deep frustration at being hindered in his mission, saying, "Wherefore we would have come unto you, even I Paul, once and again; but Satan hindered us." This statement reveals the level of opposition he faced in his ministry, an opposition not merely from physical barriers or human rejection but from spiritual forces actively working against him. One of the ways Satan tried to halt Paul's work was through slander—false accusations that attacked Paul's character and intentions, attempting to paint him as someone untrustworthy and dangerous. This slander aimed to turn people against Paul, making them question his sincerity and the truth of his message. In Acts 24:5-6, we see a vivid example of this when Paul is accused before the Roman authorities. The accusers describe him as "a pestilent fellow, and a mover of sedition among all the Jews throughout the world, and a ringleader of the sect of the Nazarenes," even claiming he attempted to "profane the temple." These accusations were intended to portray Paul as a troublemaker and a threat to both the Jewish faith and the Roman order. By calling him a "pestilent fellow," they implied that Paul was like a disease, spreading corruption and stirring up unrest wherever he went. They painted him as someone who brought division and chaos, hoping to convince the authorities that he was a danger to society. Calling him a "mover of sedition" suggested that he was a rebellious instigator, trying to incite people against established authority and cause disruption within the Jewish community and the Roman Empire. The label of "ringleader of the sect of the Nazarenes" was another attempt to slander Paul, portraying him as a leader of a suspicious and potentially dangerous religious movement. The term "sect" implied that Paul's teachings were heretical, outside the accepted norms of both Judaism and the law. By associating him with Nazareth, a place often looked down upon, they attempted to discredit both him and his followers by casting them as outsiders or people of low reputation.

Finally, the claim that he tried to "profane the temple" was a serious accusation, as the temple was the most sacred place for the Jewish people. Accusing Paul of attempting to defile it would have been shocking and offensive to many, especially to those who held the temple in high regard. This accusation was meant to stir anger and mistrust among the people, convincing them that Paul was disrespectful of their most sacred beliefs and practices. Such slander was incredibly damaging, as it not only attacked Paul's personal integrity but also cast doubt on the message he was preaching. By questioning Paul's character and his respect for religious and social order, his accusers hoped to undermine the gospel itself, leading people to reject it based on their distrust of Paul. Slander can be a powerful tool in Satan's arsenal because it spreads quickly and can create lasting damage, even if the accusations are false. People who might have been open to hearing Paul's message were likely discouraged or confused by these accusations, making them less receptive to the truth he was trying to share. Yet, despite these attacks on his character, Paul did not back down. He continued to stand firm, trusting that God would ultimately reveal the truth. Paul's response to slander was not to retaliate or become discouraged, but to rely on God for his defense. He recognized that while he might face opposition and false accusations, his mission was to serve Christ and spread the gospel, not to protect his own reputation. By staying focused on his mission and refusing to be drawn into disputes over his character, Paul set an example of humility and faithfulness. He demonstrated that when we face slander and misunderstanding, our response should be to remain faithful to God's calling and trust that He will bring justice in His own time. Paul's experience reminds us that while slander and false accusations can be painful and frustrating, they do not have the power to stop God's work. Satan may try to hinder us through lies and misrepresentation, but as long as we remain steadfast in our faith and committed to God's purpose, we can overcome these challenges. Paul's resilience in the face of slander shows us that while we may be "held back," we are never truly defeated as long as we trust in God and continue to walk in His truth.

Chapter 3 – Stoning

In I Thessalonians 2:18, Paul writes, "Wherefore we would have come unto you, even I Paul, once and again; but Satan hindered us," giving us a clear picture of the challenges he faced as he tried to fulfill his mission of spreading the gospel. One of the most intense ways Satan attempted to hinder Paul was through the physical act of stoning, a brutal form of persecution that nearly ended his life and mission. In Acts 14:19, we read of a terrifying moment when Paul's enemies stirred up a crowd to attack him violently. The verse tells us, "And there came thither certain Jews from Antioch and Iconium, who persuaded the people, and, having stoned Paul, drew him out of the city, supposing he had been dead." This event is a powerful example of the extreme lengths to which people would go to silence Paul and stop the spread of his message. The stoning was a severe and painful experience; being hit with large stones thrown at close range would have caused massive injuries, broken bones, and deep wounds. The crowd's goal was clear: they wanted to kill Paul, to eliminate him entirely so he could no longer preach about Jesus or inspire people to follow the gospel. Imagine the intensity of the pain and fear Paul must have felt as the stones struck him repeatedly, and then the darkness as he lost consciousness, left for dead. The people believed they had succeeded in their violent plan, dragging his body out of the city and leaving it there, assuming he would never get up again. To many witnesses, this seemed like the end of Paul's mission, a final and brutal end to his preaching. Satan, too, must have thought that this was a victory, a successful attempt to stop one of the most passionate and dedicated followers of Christ. Yet, Paul's story did not end there. Though he was severely wounded and beaten, he miraculously regained consciousness and, with the help of other disciples, was able to get back on his feet. Despite the pain and injuries he must have been suffering, Paul did not allow this stoning to become the final word on his mission. Instead, he showed incredible resilience and faith, choosing to continue his work even after this horrific experience. Paul's willingness to endure such suffering for the sake of the gospel is a testament to his unwavering commitment to Christ. Though Satan used the crowd's hatred and violence to hinder Paul, this stoning only strengthened Paul's resolve. His recovery and determination to keep going demonstrated to believers and unbelievers alike that no amount of persecution could stop the work of God. This stoning incident highlights the kind of trials Paul faced and the lengths to which Satan would go to try to silence him. Yet, Paul's response to this event serves as a powerful reminder that, even when we face obstacles and intense suffering, God can give us the strength to rise again and continue our journey. Paul's mission was temporarily halted, but his faith and courage allowed him to overcome even this deadly attack, showing us that while we may be "held back" by trials, we are never truly defeated as long as we trust in God's power and purpose. This story of Paul's stoning teaches us that our faith can carry us through even the most brutal opposition, and it reminds us that God's mission will continue despite any attempts by Satan to hinder it.

Chapter 4 - Shipwreck

In I Thessalonians 2:18, Paul writes, "Wherefore we would have come unto you, even I Paul, once and again; but Satan hindered us," giving us a glimpse into the immense obstacles he encountered in his efforts to spread the gospel message and minister to the early churches. Among the trials that hindered him were the perils of the sea, where Paul endured multiple shipwrecks that not only delayed his journey but also threatened his life. In 2 Corinthians 11:25, he recounts the severity of these ordeals, saying, "Thrice was I beaten with rods, once was I stoned, thrice I suffered shipwreck, a night and a day I have been in the deep." These shipwrecks were not merely minor setbacks; they were intense, life-threatening events that could have easily ended Paul's mission altogether. Imagine the terror and desperation as a ship breaks apart in a violent storm, the waves crashing down, the crew and passengers fighting to stay afloat, clinging to pieces of wood and debris in the open sea, with no land in sight and the terrifying possibility of drowning. Each shipwreck Paul endured was a harsh reminder of the dangers he faced in spreading the gospel. The physical toll of being stranded in the sea, battered by waves, and exposed to the elements for hours on end would have been exhausting and painful. Yet, despite these harrowing experiences, Paul's dedication to his mission remained unshaken. When faced with the chaotic power of nature, the fury of the storm, and the hopelessness of drifting in open water, Paul could have easily decided to turn back, to abandon the relentless travel and risk to his life. But instead, these shipwrecks became another part of his testimony of perseverance and faith. Even though these experiences delayed his journey and could have been enough to discourage anyone from continuing, Paul saw each shipwreck not as a final defeat but as an obstacle to overcome. His resilience in the face of such trials serves as an inspiration to believers, demonstrating that even when we are cast adrift, seemingly at the mercy of the elements and facing certain death, we can find strength in God to carry on. These shipwrecks were symbolic of the larger spiritual battle Paul faced, where forces beyond his control tried to steer him off course and keep him from reaching those who needed to hear the message of Christ. Satan may have used these shipwrecks to hinder Paul's journey, trying to stop him from bringing hope and salvation to others, but each time, Paul survived and continued his work. His experiences at sea, clinging to pieces of wreckage, battling exhaustion and fear, and relying on his faith to see him through, became a testament to God's sustaining power in the most desperate circumstances. Paul's determination to press on despite the danger of shipwrecks and the delays they caused reveals the depth of his commitment to his calling. While Satan sought to hinder him through these natural disasters, God's protection and purpose prevailed. Through each shipwreck, Paul's faith was refined and his resolve strengthened, proving that, while Satan may try to hold us back with the fear and turmoil of life's storms, God will not allow us to be truly defeated if we trust in His purpose and keep pressing forward. Paul's survival through multiple shipwrecks illustrates the miraculous endurance that faith can inspire, encouraging us to stay the course, even when our journey is delayed or our path becomes treacherous. Paul's story reminds us that, although we may face seemingly insurmountable obstacles, with faith, resilience, and a steadfast commitment to God's calling, we can rise above them and continue the mission set before us.

Chapter 5 – Scourging

In I Thessalonians 2:18, Paul expresses the struggles he faced in fulfilling his mission, saying, "Wherefore we would have come unto you, even I Paul, once and again; but Satan hindered us," giving us insight into the many obstacles that repeatedly blocked his path, threatening to halt his ministry. One of the most intense and painful of these hindrances was scourging, where Paul endured brutal beatings and lashings that left him physically weakened and scarred. In 2 Corinthians 11:24, he recounts this suffering, stating, "Of the Jews five times received I forty stripes save one," describing the lashes he received as punishment for his boldness in proclaiming the gospel. Each scourging was a vicious ordeal, as Paul was tied up and whipped with brutal force, each stroke tearing into his skin and leaving his body battered and bruised. The Jews had a tradition of giving forty lashes minus one, believing that forty would be too severe and might lead to death, so they reduced it by one to avoid crossing that line. Yet, even with the "forty stripes save one," the pain Paul endured was excruciating, and enduring it repeatedly would have taken a tremendous toll on his physical strength. Being scourged five times meant Paul bore lasting wounds on his back, scars that were a constant reminder of the price he paid for his faith. Such severe physical punishment was not only painful but also humiliating, as it was designed to break a person's spirit, to make them submit out of fear and exhaustion. Each time Paul was scourged, it would have taken time for his body to heal, and he would have felt the weakness and fatigue that came from such trauma. Satan surely hoped that these repeated beatings would weaken Paul to the point of giving up, making him too tired or too hurt to continue his journey. But instead of breaking him, these scourgings became symbols of Paul's incredible resilience and dedication to his mission. Despite the physical pain and weakness that followed each lashing, Paul did not let these punishments deter him from spreading the gospel. In fact, each time he recovered, he went right back to his work, preaching to new cities and encouraging believers. The scars on his body were a testament to his unwavering faith and commitment, proof that he was willing to suffer for the sake of Christ. For Paul, each scourging became another opportunity to rely on God's strength rather than his own, to show that no amount of physical pain could stop him from carrying out the purpose he believed God had set before him. He knew that, even though his body was being weakened by these beatings, his spirit was strengthened by the faith that sustained him. Paul's endurance through scourging shows us that even when we face extreme pain and hardship, we can find the strength to continue if we stay focused on our purpose and trust in God's support. Satan may have used scourging as a tool to hinder Paul's ministry, hoping that the threat of pain would keep him silent, but Paul's willingness to face this punishment over and over again demonstrates the power of faith to overcome fear and suffering. By enduring each beating and still continuing his journey, Paul showed that while his body could be wounded, his spirit remained unbreakable. His scars became symbols of his dedication, each one a mark of his loyalty to Christ and his determination to finish the work he was called to do. Through these experiences, Paul set an example for all believers, reminding us that even in times of physical weakness, when we feel beaten down by life's trials, we can still find strength in our faith. Paul's repeated scourgings did not stop him from fulfilling his mission; instead, they deepened his commitment, proving that while Satan may hinder us with pain and obstacles, he cannot defeat a heart that is fully devoted to God's purpose. Paul's story encourages us to press on, to keep moving forward even when we are weak, knowing that God can use our hardships to make us stronger and that no amount of suffering can separate us from His love or His calling. Through every scourging, Paul's faith only grew stronger, and his example continues to inspire us today, showing that true strength comes from perseverance in the face of suffering and that, even when Satan tries to hinder us with physical pain, our spirits can remain unshaken if we hold fast to our faith and trust in God's plan.

Chapter 6 – Sickness

In I Thessalonians 2:18, Paul reveals his struggle to fulfill his calling in the face of relentless obstacles, stating, "Wherefore we would have come unto you, even I Paul, once and again; but Satan hindered us." This verse hints at the hardships he encountered, and one of the most persistent and personal challenges Paul endured was his sickness—a physical infirmity that he describes as a "thorn in the flesh." In 2 Corinthians 12:7-9, Paul explains, "And lest I should be exalted above measure through the abundance of the revelations, there was given to me a thorn in the flesh, the messenger of Satan to buffet me, lest I should be exalted above measure." This mysterious "thorn" was a constant source of pain, a physical weakness that Paul recognized as something more than a mere ailment; he saw it as a direct attack on his body and spirit, something allowed by God to keep him humble. By calling it a "messenger of Satan," Paul acknowledged that this affliction was not simply an ordinary illness, but something with a spiritual dimension, a reminder of his human limitations meant to prevent pride and ensure his dependence on God. Although he prayed earnestly for God to take this burden away, Paul heard the Lord's answer in a way that transformed his understanding of weakness and strength: "My grace is sufficient for thee: for my strength is made perfect in weakness." This reply taught Paul a profound lesson, that God's grace was enough to sustain him, even when his body felt weak and his spirit felt weary. Rather than removing the thorn, God chose to empower Paul through it, allowing him to experience divine strength precisely at the points where his human strength fell short. While Satan may have intended this affliction to discourage or hinder Paul, it ultimately had the opposite effect, deepening his faith and reliance on God. Through this illness, Paul came to understand that his ministry was not built on his own abilities, resilience, or health, but on God's power working through him. Each time he felt the sting of his weakness, he was reminded of the sufficiency of God's grace, the truth that he could accomplish his mission not in spite of his weaknesses but because of them. By embracing his limitations and allowing God's power to shine through his frailties, Paul was able to press on, reaching more people with the gospel and showing that the source of his strength was not his physical body, but his unwavering trust in God's promises. His thorn in the flesh became a testament to the strength that God provides to those who trust in Him, especially in times of pain and weakness. Paul's experience with sickness teaches us that while physical ailments and limitations can feel like an unbearable burden, they can also become opportunities for spiritual growth, drawing us closer to God and allowing His power to work through us in ways we may not expect. The thorn in Paul's flesh, meant by Satan to be a hindrance, ultimately became a source of blessing as it kept Paul humble, focused on God, and reminded that true strength is found in dependence on the Lord.

Chapter 7 – Sorcery

In I Thessalonians 2:18, Paul reflects on the challenges he encountered in his mission, saying, "Wherefore we would have come unto you, even I Paul, once and again; but Satan hindered us," highlighting the numerous obstacles that attempted to prevent him from spreading the gospel. One such encounter involved sorcery and the spiritual opposition he faced from individuals who opposed his teachings. In Acts 13:8-10, we learn of Elymas the sorcerer, a man who actively sought to interfere with Paul's work. This passage describes how, while Paul and Barnabas were in Cyprus sharing the gospel, Elymas, a sorcerer and false prophet, attempted to prevent the Roman proconsul, Sergius Paulus, from accepting the faith. Elymas, whose name means "magician" or "wise man," recognized that if Sergius Paulus were to become a believer, it would impact his own influence and power. As a sorcerer, Elymas was used to manipulating people, controlling them through spells, deception, and the power of darkness. By turning people's hearts away from the truth, he kept them bound to superstition and fear. Seeing Paul and Barnabas' message as a threat to his own authority, Elymas sought to hinder them, directly opposing the work of God by trying to keep Sergius Paulus in spiritual blindness. Paul, however, filled with the Holy Spirit, saw through Elymas's schemes and confronted him boldly. In Acts 13:10, Paul rebuked him with strong words, saying, "O full of all subtilty and all mischief, thou child of the devil, thou enemy of all righteousness, wilt thou not cease to pervert the right ways of the Lord?" By calling Elymas a "child of the devil" and an "enemy of all righteousness," Paul exposed the true nature of sorcery as a force that stands against the goodness and truth of God. Paul understood that this battle was not merely a disagreement of beliefs but a deeper spiritual conflict, where the forces of light and darkness were clashing. Elymas was not simply a misguided man but a tool used by Satan to resist the spread of the gospel. When Paul spoke these words, a miraculous event occurred: Elymas was struck blind, symbolizing the spiritual blindness he inflicted on others through his deceptive practices. This temporary blindness served as a powerful sign, demonstrating the authority of God over the powers of darkness and causing Sergius Paulus to believe in the message of the gospel. Through this encounter, Paul showed that no amount of sorcery or opposition from the enemy could stand against the truth of God. Satan may have used Elymas in an attempt to hinder the spread of the gospel, but God turned this situation around, using it as an opportunity to display His power and draw Sergius Paulus to faith. Paul's confrontation with Elymas serves as a reminder of the spiritual warfare that believers face, as Satan often works through lies, deception, and fear to oppose God's work. Sorcery, in its various forms, has always been a means by which Satan tries to keep people bound, offering false promises of power and control while leading them away from the truth. Paul's experience teaches us that, while encounters with such forces can be intimidating, the power of God is greater than any spell, curse, or dark art. Paul did not back down or allow fear to silence him; instead, he stood firm in his faith, knowing that the Holy Spirit within him was far stronger than any magic or trickery that Elymas could muster. This boldness and confidence in God's power enabled Paul to overcome the obstacles set before him, showing us that we too can rely on God's strength to confront the spiritual challenges we face. Satan may attempt to hinder us through various forms of deception and opposition, but Paul's encounter with Elymas demonstrates that the truth of the gospel will always prevail. Elymas's blindness was a powerful reminder that those who seek to oppose God's work ultimately cannot see the truth themselves, and their efforts to hinder the gospel will be in vain. Paul's victory over the forces of sorcery and darkness in this encounter stands as a testament to his unwavering commitment to his mission and his trust in God's authority. While Satan may try to use sorcery, lies, or other tactics to block our path, Paul's example encourages us to stand firm, knowing that God is with us, empowering us to overcome any obstacle and ensuring that His truth will shine through in the end.

Chapter 8 – Separation

In I Thessalonians 2:18, Paul shares the frustration and longing he felt when he was prevented from visiting the believers, saying, "Wherefore we would have come unto you, even I Paul, once and again; but Satan hindered us." This verse reveals how deeply Paul cared for the churches he had helped establish, and it reflects the sorrow he felt when circumstances kept him away from these beloved communities. One of the most difficult aspects of Paul's ministry was the separation he often experienced from the churches and people he loved. In Romans 1:13, he expresses a similar sentiment, writing, "Now I would not have you ignorant, brethren, that oftentimes I purposed to come unto you, but was let hitherto," showing that his desire to visit the Romans was sincere and long-standing, yet something repeatedly stood in his way. This separation was not just a matter of physical distance; it was a deep emotional burden for Paul, who wanted nothing more than to encourage, teach, and strengthen the believers in person. For Paul, being separated from the churches he cared for felt like an obstacle that prevented him from fully fulfilling his calling, as he longed to be with them, share in their struggles, and help them grow in their faith. The distance was painful, especially when he knew that many of these churches were young and faced their own hardships, needing guidance and encouragement that he could provide. Paul's letters, though powerful, were only a partial substitute for his presence, and he knew that writing to them could not fully replace the impact of being there in person, praying with them, teaching them directly, and comforting them in their trials. Separation was a unique kind of suffering for Paul, as he often felt that his absence might leave the believers vulnerable to false teachings, persecution, and doubt. He wanted to be there to protect them, to correct misunderstandings, and to encourage them to stay strong, but time and again, he found himself hindered from visiting them as he wished. This separation was a persistent reminder that his ministry was not in his control but depended on God's timing and purpose. Even though he could not always be with the churches in person, Paul trusted that God would protect and guide them, filling in the gaps that his absence created. The letters he wrote, including those to the Romans and Thessalonians, became lifelines for these early Christians, carrying messages of hope, instruction, and encouragement across the miles. These letters reveal Paul's heart, his longing to see the churches flourish, and his unwavering commitment to support them however he could, despite the physical barriers that separated them. Though he felt the pain of separation deeply, Paul used every opportunity to stay connected, finding ways to guide them from afar and trusting that God would work through his words, even if he couldn't be there in person. This experience of separation taught Paul valuable lessons about patience, reliance on God, and the power of prayer. He knew that while he might be separated from the believers in body, they were united in spirit, all part of the same body of Christ, and he prayed for them constantly, lifting up their needs to God and asking for strength and protection on their behalf. Paul's letters often mention these prayers, showing his ongoing care and dedication, and reminding the believers that even in his absence, he was with them in heart and spirit. This separation also showed Paul and the early church that the gospel was not limited by physical distance; it could spread and thrive even when the apostles were not physically present. In fact, Paul's letters, born out of the necessity created by separation, became foundational texts for Christian faith, containing timeless teachings that have guided believers for generations. What seemed like a hindrance actually served a greater purpose, as these letters reached beyond the original recipients, strengthening believers across the world and throughout history. Paul's longing to visit the churches, combined with the reality of separation, became a testimony of his love and dedication to the gospel, proving that his commitment to the faith was unwavering, regardless of the obstacles in his way. Though Satan may have tried to hinder Paul by keeping him physically distant from these communities, God used that separation to accomplish even greater things, turning Paul's letters into instruments of encouragement, correction, and inspiration that would endure far beyond his lifetime. Through this experience, Paul demonstrated that true connection and support are not bound by physical presence, and that the bonds of Christian fellowship can overcome even the greatest distances. His separation from the churches he loved served as a powerful example of how faith, prayer, and perseverance can bridge any gap, proving that while Satan may try to hold us back or create barriers, God's purpose will always find a way through.

Chapter 9 - Seduction of Converts

IN I THESSALONIANS 2:18, Paul expresses the frustration and sorrow he felt at being prevented from visiting the believers, saying, "Wherefore we would have come unto you, even I Paul, once and again; but Satan hindered us." This verse gives us a glimpse of the challenges Paul faced as he worked tirelessly to guide and protect the early Christians. One of the greatest threats to his mission and to the faith of the believers was the seduction of converts—the dangerous influence of false teachers who led new believers astray and spread confusion among the churches. Paul was deeply concerned about these false teachings and the effect they had on young Christians, whose faith was still growing and who were especially vulnerable to deceit. In 2 Corinthians 11:3-4, Paul warns the believers about this, saying, "But I fear, lest by any means, as the serpent beguiled Eve through his subtilty, so your minds should be corrupted from the simplicity that is in Christ. For if he that cometh preacheth another Jesus, whom we have not preached, or if ye receive another spirit, which ye have not received, or another gospel, which ye have not accepted, ye might well bear with him." Here, Paul compares the deception of these false teachers to the cunning serpent in the Garden of Eden, who seduced Eve with subtle lies and led her away from God's truth. Paul feared that these false teachers would do the same to the converts he had worked so hard to nurture in the faith, slowly corrupting their minds and drawing them away from the purity and simplicity of the gospel. These false teachers often came with messages that sounded appealing and persuasive, mixing truth with lies to create a version of the gospel that suited their own interests. They would preach "another Jesus" or offer "another spirit," confusing the believers and making them question what Paul had taught them. For new converts, this was especially dangerous, as they were still learning the foundations of their faith and might not yet have the spiritual maturity to discern truth from deception. Paul saw this seduction as a direct attack from Satan, who used these false teachers to try and undo the work of the gospel, creating division, doubt, and chaos within the church. The seduction of converts was a painful and frustrating obstacle for Paul, as he felt a deep responsibility to protect these new believers, yet often found himself hindered from being physically present to guide them. This separation made it difficult for him to confront the false teachers directly, and so he relied on his letters to warn the churches and remind them of the true gospel. Paul's words in his letters became his means of battling these false teachings, urging the believers to hold fast to the truth and resist the lure of doctrines that sounded appealing but were not aligned with Christ's message. He reminded them that the gospel was simple and pure, rooted in the life, death, and resurrection of Jesus, and that any teaching that strayed from this core truth was not from God. Paul's dedication to preserving the truth of the gospel was unwavering, even when he was frustrated by his inability to be there in person. His letters served as a shield, helping to guard the minds and hearts of the believers against the seduction of false teachings. Paul knew that his absence made the believers more vulnerable, as they could not receive his guidance and reassurance face-to-face, but he trusted that God would protect them and give them the discernment they needed to recognize the truth. Through his letters, Paul encouraged the churches to stay vigilant, to test the teachings they heard, and to cling to the message he had shared with them, which came directly from Christ. He urged them to remember that the gospel was not about complex philosophies or enticing words but about the transformative power of God's love and grace. Paul's struggle with the seduction of converts and the presence of false teachers reveals the depth of his love for the early Christians and his commitment to their spiritual growth. He knew that these new believers were at a critical stage in their faith journey and that the wrong influences could lead them away from the path of truth. Paul's letters became lifelines, reminding the believers that even though he was not there with them, they had the teachings of Christ to rely on, and he encouraged them to hold on to this truth, no matter what other messages they might hear. Through his dedication and perseverance, Paul showed that while false teachings and the seduction of converts posed serious threats, the power of the gospel and the guidance of the Holy Spirit were more than enough to overcome them. His example teaches us the importance of standing firm in our faith, staying rooted in the simplicity of Christ's message, and being wary of anything that might lead us away from the truth. Satan's attempt to hinder Paul through the influence of false teachers ultimately could not succeed, for Paul's words continued to reach the believers, strengthening them in faith and equipping them to resist any teachings that did not align with the gospel. Paul's struggle with the seduction of converts serves as a powerful reminder that, though we may face many distractions and challenges in our faith journey, the truth of Christ will always be our anchor, guiding us through the storms of deception and keeping us close to God's heart. Through his relentless efforts, Paul safeguarded the early church, ensuring that the gospel remained pure, and he inspires us today to stay true to the message of Christ, even when other voices try to lead us astray.

Chapter 10 - Stiff Opposition

In I Thessalonians 2:18, Paul reveals the challenges he faced in trying to visit and encourage the believers, saying, "Wherefore we would have come unto you, even I Paul, once and again; but Satan hindered us." This verse shows that Paul encountered many barriers in his efforts to spread the gospel, and one of the most persistent and dangerous obstacles he faced was stiff opposition from religious leaders who resisted his preaching. This resistance often turned into outright hostility, as these leaders felt threatened by Paul's message of salvation through Christ, a message that challenged their traditions and authority. In Acts 9:23, we see an example of this fierce opposition, as it states, "And after that many days were fulfilled, the Jews took counsel to kill him." This verse paints a clear picture of the danger Paul faced, as the Jewish leaders went so far as to plot his death to silence him. They saw Paul as a threat to their beliefs and way of life, as he preached that Jesus was the Messiah and that salvation was available to all through faith, not by the law alone. To them, Paul's teachings were radical, undermining the authority they held over the people and challenging the established religious practices. They feared that Paul's influence would grow, leading people away from the old traditions and toward this new path of faith in Christ. The religious leaders were determined to stop him at any cost, using their power and influence to incite opposition, stir up crowds, and even coordinate assassination attempts. The resistance Paul encountered was not merely a matter of theological disagreement; it was a fierce, sometimes violent rejection of the message of grace he proclaimed. Everywhere Paul went, he faced the risk of confrontation with religious authorities who sought to discredit him, disrupt his work, and, when possible, end his life. This opposition was a constant reminder that his mission was not only about spreading good news but also about standing firm against forces that sought to maintain control over the people's beliefs. Despite knowing the dangers he faced, Paul never allowed this opposition to deter him from his mission. He knew that his calling to preach Christ was more important than his personal safety, and he was willing to risk everything to fulfill that calling. The stiff opposition only strengthened Paul's resolve, as he saw each challenge as an opportunity to prove the truth and power of the gospel. Even when religious leaders plotted to kill him, as they did in Damascus, Paul found a way to escape, continuing his journey and preaching with even greater determination. The fierce opposition he encountered served to highlight the courage and resilience of his faith, showing others that he believed in the message of Christ so deeply that he was willing to face death for it. This resistance from religious leaders was part of the spiritual battle Paul often referenced, a battle not just against flesh and blood, but against the powers and principalities that sought to keep people in darkness. For Paul, each instance of opposition from religious authorities was a reminder that Satan was actively working to hinder the spread of the gospel, using those in positions of power to create obstacles and instill fear. But Paul refused to back down, drawing strength from his trust in God and his conviction that the message of Christ was worth any sacrifice. His encounters with religious leaders who opposed him became part of his testimony, showing that no amount of human authority could stop the work of God. Paul's willingness to face this opposition with courage and faith set an example for the early believers, encouraging them to stand firm in their own faith, even when faced with similar resistance. His life demonstrated that, although religious leaders and others in power might try to hinder the gospel, God's purpose would ultimately prevail. Paul's resilience in the face of stiff opposition inspires us today, reminding us that the truth of Christ cannot be silenced, no matter how strong the opposition may seem. Through every challenge, Paul's faith grew stronger, and his determination to preach the gospel only increased, proving that while Satan may try to hinder us, he cannot overcome those who are committed to God's calling.

Chapter 11 - Seizure by Authorities

Paul's life as a follower of Jesus Christ was full of constant dangers, risks, and hardships, yet he faced these with unwavering dedication to his mission of sharing the Gospel. His calling was clear: to preach Christ, whether people received him gladly or met him with hostility, whether doors opened easily or authorities slammed them shut. Time and again, Paul encountered opposition that was fierce, often from influential leaders, both Jewish and Gentile, who saw his message as a threat to their beliefs and social order. His ministry often seemed to be in danger, interrupted by threats and arrests, making it evident that there was a price to pay for proclaiming the message of salvation. Paul himself wrote about these hindrances, expressing the sorrow and frustration he felt in 1 Thessalonians 2:18, saying, "Wherefore we would have come unto you, even I Paul, once and again; but Satan hindered us." To understand the extent of Paul's struggles, we must consider his imprisonment at Philippi, described in Acts 16:23, as an example of the "seizure by authorities" that interrupted his work for Christ. Paul and Silas, in obedience to God's calling, had come to Philippi and preached by the riverside, where many had gathered. Their words inspired and drew the attention of the people, but it wasn't long before the authorities noticed. When they cast a spirit of divination out of a slave girl, angered locals dragged Paul and Silas before the magistrates. The crowd quickly turned against them, accusing them of troubling the city and teaching customs that were not lawful for Romans to observe. Without a fair hearing, the authorities commanded that they be beaten with rods, a brutal punishment meant to instill fear and submission. After many stripes were laid upon them, Paul and Silas were thrown into the inner prison, their feet fastened in stocks. The physical pain and confinement could have easily discouraged them, but instead, their response showed their unbreakable faith. Despite the dark prison and the unjust treatment, they chose to praise God, praying and singing hymns in the dead of night. Their joy and trust in God were so powerful that it filled the prison, impacting the other prisoners who listened. This spirit of praise and resilience revealed how deeply rooted their faith was. They understood that their calling was worth more than comfort or freedom, and even in chains, they saw an opportunity to glorify God. In response to their faithfulness, God sent an earthquake that shook the prison's foundations, opening all doors and loosening everyone's bonds. The jailer, terrified that the prisoners had escaped and that his life was at risk, was about to take his own life. But Paul's cry of reassurance, "Do thyself no harm: for we are all here," changed everything. Instead of fleeing, Paul saw an opportunity to share the Gospel, leading the jailer and his family to Christ. This moment turned what could have been a story of defeat into one of victory for the Gospel. Although the authorities had intended to silence Paul and stop the spread of his message, God had used this very trial to spread His word even further. This experience at Philippi was only one of many times Paul would find himself in the hands of authorities who sought to interrupt his ministry. In Jerusalem, he was once again seized and falsely accused of bringing Gentiles into the temple, leading to another arrest. As Paul stood trial before rulers and kings, such as Felix, Festus, and Agrippa, he didn't shrink back or compromise. Instead, he boldly testified of his faith, using these moments to share the message of salvation even with the leaders who held his fate in their hands. Each trial and imprisonment provided an unexpected platform for Paul to speak of Jesus Christ, and he took every opportunity to proclaim that he was not ashamed of the Gospel. His imprisonments became occasions to witness to guards, fellow prisoners, and officials who might never have heard about Jesus otherwise. In fact, many of his letters, like Ephesians, Philippians, Colossians, and Philemon, were written from prison. These "prison epistles" reached churches and believers throughout the Roman Empire, spreading words of encouragement, doctrine, and faith. Paul's letters often reminded his readers that, although he was bound in chains, the Word of God was not bound. His teachings, inspired and written during his imprisonment, carried a powerful message of hope and resilience that encouraged the early Christians to remain faithful even in persecution. His example showed them that no earthly authority could truly hinder God's work, for the Gospel would continue to flourish regardless of opposition. Each trial Paul endured was a testament to his unwavering commitment to Christ, teaching believers that faith does not waver in the face of adversity. Rather, it grows stronger, as faith refined by fire becomes an even brighter witness to the world. Paul's repeated imprisonments, far from being a mere interruption to his ministry, became a central part of his testimony. In chains, he experienced God's power and presence in profound ways, discovering that God's strength was made perfect in his weakness. He famously wrote, "For to me to live is Christ, and to die is gain," showing that his dedication to Christ was stronger than any fear of suffering or death. He knew that his purpose was to serve God wholeheartedly, even if it meant facing frequent arrests and mistreatment. Through every hardship, Paul demonstrated that suffering for the sake of Christ was a privilege, not a burden. He did not consider himself a victim of circumstance, but rather a willing servant, committed to following wherever God led him. His imprisonments showed that true freedom is found not in escaping trials but in remaining faithful amid them. This powerful message resonates with believers who, like Paul, may face opposition or persecution for their faith. Paul's story encourages Christians to stand firm, for he showed that every difficulty could be an opportunity to share the love and truth of Christ. His life was a testimony that no earthly authority, no matter how powerful, could extinguish the light of the Gospel. His story reminds us that God can use even the harshest circumstances for His glory, turning prisons into places of worship, trials into testimonies, and hardships into hope. Through Paul's sufferings, believers are encouraged to trust in God's purpose, knowing that He is with them in every situation, and that He can use every moment, even those that seem like interruptions, to fulfill His plan.

Chapter 12 - Sleepless Nights

Paul's life and ministry were full of exhausting challenges, and one of the most striking hardships he faced was the constant strain that led to countless sleepless nights. Paul wrote in 2 Corinthians 11:27, "In weariness and painfulness, in watchings often, in hunger and thirst, in fastings often, in cold and nakedness," describing the toll that his work and the threats against him took on his body and spirit. Paul's commitment to spreading the Gospel was unwavering, even when it meant pushing himself beyond physical limits and enduring long nights without rest. Sleeplessness became a frequent companion in his ministry, as his heart was burdened for the churches he had founded, the new believers he encouraged, and the lost souls he tirelessly sought to reach. Every city he visited held new challenges, dangers, and threats, from opposition by religious leaders to persecution by local authorities. Yet Paul kept going, driven by a passion to see the Gospel spread far and wide. Night after night, Paul would find himself awake, sometimes praying for strength, sometimes writing letters of encouragement, and other times watching for the dangers that lurked nearby. Paul's sleepless nights were not only from physical threats but from the inner burdens he carried for the believers. He felt responsible for their spiritual growth, often worrying for their faith under persecution. In 2 Corinthians 11:28, he wrote, "Beside those things that are without, that which cometh upon me daily, the care of all the churches." His sleepless nights reflected the depth of his concern, knowing that these believers needed guidance, strength, and encouragement to stand firm. When Paul was not able to sleep, he would use those hours to pray, interceding on behalf of each church, each congregation, each person he had come to love in Christ. Despite his physical exhaustion, Paul found spiritual strength in these nights, pouring his heart out to God for the churches. The weight of the mission, combined with the constant threats against him, tested Paul's endurance to its limits. He would press on, traveling great distances by land and sea, often finding himself in dangerous situations that robbed him of peace and rest. Yet, even on nights filled with watchfulness and tension, Paul did not lose hope. He learned to rely on God's strength when his own strength had run out. He understood that his sleepless nights were part of his calling, a necessary sacrifice for the sake of the Gospel. Paul's exhaustion only served to show the depth of his dedication; he willingly endured sleeplessness and fatigue so that he could be a light to those in darkness. His sleepless nights were not wasted, for each one strengthened his resolve to carry on, no matter how tired he felt. Paul's life was an example of selfless commitment, teaching believers that faith often requires sacrifice, that true love for God's work does not stop when tiredness sets in. Even in moments when sleep would have been a relief, Paul chose to push through, showing that his mission was more important than his comfort. He understood that every hour, even sleepless ones, could be used for God's glory.

Chapter 13 – Starvation

Paul's life as a servant of Christ was marked by countless hardships, and among the most grueling was his experience of starvation and hunger as he traveled to spread the Gospel. In 2 Corinthians 11:27, Paul wrote about his struggles, saying, "In weariness and painfulness, in watchings often, in hunger and thirst, in fastings often, in cold and nakedness." Hunger was not just an occasional discomfort for Paul; it was a frequent reality as he traveled across cities and regions with few resources and little assurance of where his next meal would come from. Paul's journey to share the message of salvation led him to remote places and hostile environments, where food and supplies were scarce, and support was limited. Unlike today, where resources are more accessible, Paul's time was one of limited means, especially for those proclaiming a new and controversial faith. Yet Paul was not deterred by his physical hunger, viewing it as part of the sacrifice he willingly made to fulfill his calling. Hunger became a companion, a silent reminder of the cost of following Christ wholeheartedly. There were days when he would go without food, either due to lack of provision or because he was so engrossed in his mission that he did not pause to eat. Every pang of hunger served as a physical reminder of his dependence on God, pushing Paul to trust that God would provide in His own time. Paul's experiences with starvation also came from times when he chose to fast and pray, seeking God's guidance and strength above earthly sustenance. In these moments, he set aside his need for food, desiring to draw closer to God even at the expense of his physical needs. But fasting was not the only cause of his hunger; there were times he simply had no food because he was cut off from resources, isolated by persecution, or lacking funds to buy necessities. Traveling through ancient cities and regions meant that food was not always available, especially for someone often seen as an outsider or even a threat by those in power. The authorities, both Jewish and Roman, saw Paul's teachings as a challenge to their traditions and authority, often forcing him to flee or live in secrecy. In these times of escape, hiding, or imprisonment, he faced hunger not as a choice but as a reality of his mission. His dedication to the Gospel meant that his own comfort and survival were secondary to the spread of the message of Christ. Paul's experience of hunger went beyond mere physical deprivation; it was an exercise in patience, faith, and endurance. Each time he found himself without food, he was reminded of Jesus' own words that "man shall not live by bread alone, but by every word that proceedeth out of the mouth of God" (Matthew 4:4). This verse likely strengthened Paul, helping him see that even in his moments of physical weakness, he was spiritually sustained by God's promises. Hunger humbled Paul, teaching him that his strength was not in physical provisions but in his dependence on God. The lack of food became a testament to his resilience, showing others that nothing—not even starvation—could shake his commitment to Christ. Paul's resilience in the face of starvation inspired early believers who read his letters or heard of his sacrifices. Knowing that Paul endured hunger for the Gospel encouraged them to press on through their own struggles, reminding them that God could use even the most difficult circumstances for His glory. Hunger, which would have broken many, became a powerful part of Paul's testimony, proving that his devotion was genuine and unwavering. Paul's letters, written during these times of hardship, often spoke of joy and contentment, showing that his satisfaction was found in Christ alone. Starvation did not weaken his spirit but rather strengthened it, making him a powerful witness to the strength and hope that faith in Christ provides. Paul's willingness to endure starvation set an example for believers, teaching them that dedication to God's mission might require them to sacrifice comfort, security, and even basic needs. His life demonstrated that true faith endures hardship, trusting in God's provision and care, no matter the physical circumstances. Paul's experiences with hunger were part of the greater story of his ministry, illustrating a life fully surrendered to God's calling. He showed that the pursuit of God's kingdom was worth any sacrifice, even starvation, as it opened the door for countless others to hear the Gospel and be saved. Through his struggles, Paul displayed the true cost of discipleship, inspiring believers then and now to find strength, not in earthly provisions, but in the eternal promise of God's love and provision.

Chapter 14 – Surveillance

Paul's ministry was marked by relentless challenges, and one of the most intense forms of opposition he faced was constant surveillance and monitoring by his enemies, who sought any chance to hinder his work and even take his life. Throughout his journeys, Paul was under close watch, especially by those who feared the transformative power of his message about Jesus Christ. His story is full of instances where enemies plotted against him, watched his every move, and waited for an opportunity to capture or kill him, as they viewed him as a dangerous threat to their religious traditions and social order. Acts 9:24 gives us one example: shortly after Paul's conversion, when he began preaching Christ openly, the Jews plotted to kill him, watching the city gates day and night to seize him. Paul's sudden shift from a persecutor of Christians to a follower of Jesus alarmed the Jewish leaders, who quickly recognized the influence and passion he brought to this new mission. To them, Paul was a symbol of betrayal and danger; he was once a devout Pharisee, but now he proclaimed the very message he had once condemned. Determined to stop him, these leaders set up a watch around the city, hoping to trap him when he attempted to leave. However, Paul's disciples helped him escape by lowering him in a basket through an opening in the wall, allowing him to avoid capture and continue his ministry. This kind of surveillance and monitoring became a recurring theme in Paul's life. Each new city presented similar risks, with authorities, local religious leaders, and sometimes even mobs watching him closely, ready to turn him over to the authorities or worse. From Jerusalem to Damascus, Philippi to Thessalonica, Paul lived under the shadow of constant watchfulness. His enemies saw him as a threat, a disruptor who dared to challenge established beliefs, and they used every means possible to monitor him, seeking opportunities to stop him permanently. Paul's understanding of this constant surveillance was part of the "hindrance" he mentioned in I Thessalonians 2:18, when he said, "Wherefore we would have come unto you, even I Paul, once and again; but Satan hindered us." Paul understood that the opposition he faced was not just a matter of human plotting but was rooted in spiritual warfare, with Satan using these people to hinder the spread of the Gospel. Surveillance, then, was not only physical but also a spiritual threat, a reminder that his mission would constantly be met with resistance. Knowing he was being watched, Paul often had to move cautiously and rely on the support of fellow believers who provided shelter, warnings, and sometimes, as in Damascus, creative escape plans. His movements were strategic, sometimes secretive, and always driven by his reliance on God's guidance. This constant monitoring could have caused him to live in fear, but Paul chose instead to live with boldness. His resolve was unshakable, knowing that the message he carried was more powerful than any scheme devised against him. Paul's letters reveal that he was aware of the surveillance but undeterred by it, viewing these trials as a way to demonstrate the endurance and courage that come from faith. In fact, Paul often turned these situations into opportunities to share the Gospel with those who guarded him or monitored his actions. When he was eventually arrested and placed under house arrest in Rome, his "surveillance" included guards who would hear him preach and see his unwavering faith up close. Many came to faith through Paul's influence, proving that even constant monitoring could not silence the truth he shared. Paul's life was a testament to the fact that God's work cannot be stopped by human or spiritual opposition. Every city he entered, every guard assigned to him, every enemy who watched his movements only served to spread his testimony further. His response to surveillance showed believers that they could live boldly and courageously for Christ, even when under scrutiny. Paul's life was a witness to the power of God, for even those who monitored him could not ignore his faith. Through his endurance, Paul taught that surveillance and monitoring, rather than hindering God's mission, became a part of his testimony to God's sustaining power and purpose, reaching even those who sought to silence him.

Chapter 15 – Schemes

Paul's journey as a servant of Christ was fraught with peril, and one of the greatest dangers he faced came from the countless schemes and plots formed against him by both Jews and Gentiles who saw his message as a threat to their power and beliefs. In Acts 23:12-13, we see one particularly chilling plot: a group of more than forty Jews, driven by hatred for Paul and what he stood for, made a solemn vow neither to eat nor drink until they had killed him. This conspiracy was no mere threat; these men were deadly serious, united in their determination to silence Paul permanently, and they devised a scheme to ambush him on his way to the council. This was only one of many instances in which Paul's life was targeted. From the moment of his conversion on the road to Damascus, Paul faced intense opposition. Once a respected Pharisee, Paul's transformation into a bold preacher of Christ unsettled the religious leaders, who felt betrayed by his shift from upholding the Jewish law to proclaiming Jesus as the Messiah. Their fury was relentless, and they stirred up others to act against him, enlisting mobs and manipulating authorities to carry out their plots. Gentile leaders and influential citizens were also disturbed by Paul's message, as it threatened their customs, idol worship, and economic systems. In cities like Ephesus, where silversmiths profiting from idols felt their livelihood was endangered, Paul became a target. Both Jews and Gentiles, with their own reasons for disliking Paul's teachings, found common ground in their opposition to him, seeing him as a threat to their way of life. Throughout his ministry, Paul was often forced to escape under the cover of darkness, lowering himself in baskets from city walls or fleeing quickly to evade those who sought to kill him. Each city brought new dangers and new schemes, from Thessalonica to Jerusalem. These plots were not just human conspiracies; Paul recognized the hand of Satan in the constant opposition he faced, as he expressed in I Thessalonians 2:18: "Wherefore we would have come unto you, even I Paul, once and again; but Satan hindered us."

Paul understood that these schemes were part of a larger spiritual battle, and his enemies were tools used by Satan to try to thwart the spread of the Gospel. Despite these plots, Paul pressed on, trusting that God was with him, protecting and guiding him through every scheme meant to harm him. His life was filled with close encounters, from nearly being stoned to death in Lystra to narrowly escaping assassination in Jerusalem. Yet, each plot only strengthened his resolve, for Paul saw every escape, every act of God's protection, as evidence that his mission was blessed by God. He continued to preach boldly, refusing to let fear of schemes and plots silence him. Paul's unwavering commitment became a powerful example to early believers, teaching them that no scheme of man or plot of the enemy could overpower the will of God. His survival, despite so many threats, was a testimony to God's sovereign protection, inspiring believers to remain steadfast. Paul's story shows that while the world may plot and scheme, God's purposes cannot be thwarted. Every attempt on his life only furthered the spread of the Gospel, reaching new places and people. His life reveals that schemes of harm are powerless before God's plans, for He uses even the plots of enemies to fulfill His purposes. Through Paul's perseverance, we learn that no scheme can stand against the resolve of a servant of Christ who is protected by God's hand, a lesson that strengthens believers to trust in God's provision amid any threat

Chapter 16 - Slanderous Rumors

Paul's ministry was continually shadowed by slanderous rumors and false accusations, and these persistent rumors aimed to undermine his teachings, causing confusion and mistrust among the early believers he sought to strengthen in their faith. In Galatians 1:7, Paul addressed this issue directly, saying, "Which is not another; but there be some that trouble you, and would pervert the gospel of Christ." These rumors were often spread by individuals who opposed Paul's teachings and sought to twist the Gospel message, presenting a distorted version of the truth. These false teachers spread lies that Paul's message of salvation through faith in Jesus Christ alone was misleading, and they insisted that believers still had to follow the Jewish law to be saved. This falsehood troubled the new believers, especially those in Galatia, where Paul had preached the freedom and grace found in Christ. These rumors didn't just challenge his teachings; they attacked his character, calling into question his authority as an apostle and his motives. Some accused him of changing his message to please people or of preaching an incomplete Gospel to win favor. Others falsely claimed that Paul was against the law and disrespectful of Jewish traditions, painting him as a traitor to his heritage. This constant slander was exhausting for Paul, as he cared deeply for the believers he had led to Christ, and seeing them misled by false teachings caused him great pain. Paul knew that these rumors were not just harmless gossip but strategic lies meant to disrupt the unity and growth of the church, aiming to pull people away from the truth of the Gospel. These accusations also created distrust between Paul and the churches he founded, forcing him to defend his calling and remind them of his sincerity and sacrifice in spreading the Gospel. This battle against slander was not a simple matter; it required Paul to repeatedly clarify his teachings, write letters to address misunderstandings, and encourage believers to hold fast to the true Gospel. His letters to the churches, like those to the Galatians and Corinthians, often addressed these rumors head-on, affirming his authority and the truth of the message he preached. He reminded them that his calling came directly from Christ, not from men, and that he was not trying to please people but was wholly committed to serving God. Despite his efforts, the rumors persisted, showing that his enemies were relentless in their mission to undermine him. These slanderous rumors spread far and wide, fueled by those who opposed the message of grace, preferring the old system of laws and traditions that placed heavy burdens on the people. Paul's message of freedom in Christ threatened those who held power through religious rules, so they tried to discredit him by spreading lies. Paul's response to these accusations was a model of patience and clarity, as he continued to teach the Gospel boldly, reminding the believers of the truth and encouraging them to stay firm in their faith. He trusted that God would reveal the truth and that his integrity would shine through despite the lies against him. Paul's experience with slander taught early Christians an important lesson: that following Christ often means facing opposition, even from within religious circles, and that they must be discerning and steadfast in their faith. These false rumors, though aimed to harm, could not destroy Paul's commitment, for he saw them as part of the spiritual battle against the spread of the Gospel. His perseverance in the face of slander serves as an inspiration to believers, showing that rumors and lies, no matter how persistent, cannot weaken a true servant of God who is rooted in the truth. Paul's faithfulness amidst slander reveals that the power of the Gospel is stronger than any rumor, and that God's truth will ultimately prevail, even when faced with false accusations. His life encourages believers to stand firm, knowing that slander and opposition may come, but that the truth of Christ remains unshaken, enduring beyond any rumor or false claim

Chapter 17 – Scorn

Paul's journey of spreading the Gospel was marked by many hardships, and one of the most painful trials he faced was the constant scorn, mockery, and contempt from those who rejected the message of Jesus Christ. His experiences were not just moments of misunderstanding; they were deep and often humiliating encounters where people openly ridiculed him and the faith he preached. In Acts 17:32, we see an example of this scorn when Paul spoke in Athens at Mars Hill, where the philosophers and scholars gathered to discuss new ideas. Paul passionately presented the truth of the resurrection of Jesus, but instead of accepting or even considering his words with respect, many openly mocked him. The text says, "And when they heard of the resurrection of the dead, some mocked." This scorn was not an isolated incident in Paul's life; rather, it was a recurring theme throughout his ministry. As he traveled from city to city, Paul encountered people who dismissed him as a fool or worse. His message of a crucified and risen Savior was seen as absurd to the Greek philosophers, who valued human wisdom, and offensive to the Jewish leaders, who could not accept a Messiah who suffered and died on a cross. Paul's teachings challenged the pride and beliefs of those who clung to the ways of the world, and as a result, he was often met with laughter, insults, and contempt. This mockery was not easy for Paul, as he deeply cared for the souls of those who were rejecting the truth, knowing the consequences of unbelief. He felt a profound burden for every city he entered, hoping to reach both Jew and Gentile alike with the hope of salvation, but instead of acceptance, he was often met with sneers. People would call him a "babbler" or accuse him of trying to introduce strange gods, showing disdain not just for his message but for his character. The pain of such rejection, knowing that many were choosing to remain in spiritual darkness, weighed heavily on Paul, yet he continued steadfastly, determined not to let mockery stop him from fulfilling his mission. This scorn was, in many ways, a test of Paul's resolve and faith, as he faced the same mockery that Jesus Himself endured. Paul understood that standing for the truth often meant facing rejection, and he embraced this scorn as part of his calling. He wrote to the Corinthians that "the preaching of the cross is to them that perish foolishness" (1 Corinthians 1:18), acknowledging that many would see the message of Christ as foolish, but he was not ashamed. Paul's boldness in the face of ridicule served as a powerful example to early believers, showing them that they, too, might face scorn and contempt for their faith but that they should not be discouraged. The mockery only strengthened Paul's conviction, for he saw that the world's laughter was a temporary response, while the truth of the Gospel held eternal power. His experiences teach us that the call to follow Christ often means standing firm against the world's scorn, trusting that God's approval is worth more than human acceptance. Even as people laughed and turned away, Paul knew that some would believe, and he held on to that hope, knowing that every effort, every moment of endurance, had eternal significance. His willingness to bear the shame and rejection associated with the Gospel encourages believers to be courageous, to speak the truth boldly, and to understand that mockery is not a defeat but a part of walking in faith. Paul's life and his response to scorn remind us that the Gospel, though met with mockery, remains the power of God unto salvation for those who believe. His example calls us to stand firm, to love those who reject us, and to continue sharing the truth, no matter the contempt we might face, for in God's eyes, faithfulness is what truly matters. Paul's steadfastness in the face of scorn reflects the strength of his commitment and the depth of his love for Christ, encouraging all believers to keep the faith, even when the world laughs, knowing that God's truth will ultimately triumph over every mocking voice.

Chapter 18 - Subversion of Message

Paul's mission to spread the Gospel of Jesus Christ was constantly under attack, and one of the greatest challenges he faced was the subversion of his message by others who preached distorted versions of the truth he had worked so tirelessly to share. This problem weighed heavily on his heart, as he had poured his life into teaching the pure message of salvation through faith in Jesus alone, only to see others come behind him, twisting his words and adding their own ideas. In Galatians 1:6-9, Paul expressed his distress over this issue, saying, "I marvel that ye are so soon removed from him that called you into the grace of Christ unto another gospel: which is not another; but there be some that trouble you, and would pervert the gospel of Christ. But though we, or an angel from heaven, preach any other gospel unto you than that which we have preached unto you, let him be accursed." Paul's frustration was clear, as he saw that some people were using his teachings but adding requirements, like the need to follow Jewish laws, that were not part of the true Gospel. These distortions turned the free gift of grace into something that people felt they had to earn, robbing the Gospel of its power and simplicity. Paul knew that the message of Christ was meant to bring freedom from the law's demands, yet false teachers were spreading a version of the Gospel that burdened believers with rules and regulations that Jesus had already fulfilled on their behalf. This subversion of the message was not a minor issue for Paul; it was a spiritual battle, as he recognized that Satan was using these distortions to confuse and mislead new believers. Each time he left a city after preaching, he would later hear reports that certain individuals had come in and altered his teachings, leaving the people questioning what was truly required of them. The addition of these false teachings turned the Gospel into a mix of grace and works, leading people to believe they needed to earn God's favor. This corruption of the message broke Paul's heart, as he had labored tirelessly to preach Christ alone, emphasizing that salvation came not by works of the law but by faith in the sacrifice Jesus made. Paul's letters to churches like those in Galatia were written with urgency, correcting the misunderstandings that had taken root and pleading with the believers to hold fast to the original message they had received. He reminded them that anyone preaching a different Gospel was misleading them, and he went as far as to pronounce a curse on those who perverted the message of grace. Paul's warnings about distorted teachings were strong because he understood the eternal stakes; he knew that a twisted Gospel could lead people away from true salvation, replacing faith with fear and grace with bondage. His words were meant to protect the early Christians from falling into the trap of legalism or being led astray by those who seemed persuasive but were ultimately false teachers. Paul's stance showed his deep love and care for the believers, as he was willing to confront the false teachers and call out their errors to protect the purity of the Gospel. This struggle against the subversion of his message was an ongoing challenge throughout Paul's ministry, as he traveled from city to city, establishing churches and then later hearing reports of how others had tried to reshape his teachings. Yet Paul remained steadfast, continually urging the believers to remember the true Gospel, to hold on to the grace of Christ, and to reject any additions or alterations. His letters, such as those to the Galatians, became a defense of the Gospel, calling out the dangers of any teaching that added to or took away from the message of Christ crucified and risen. Paul's warnings still resonate today, reminding believers to be vigilant, to study the Scriptures, and to ensure that the Gospel they follow is the pure truth of God's Word. His perseverance in defending the message of grace showed that he valued the truth above all else and that he would not allow anyone to distort or dilute the message of salvation. Paul's response to these false teachings teaches us the importance of guarding the Gospel, understanding its core, and refusing to compromise its truth. He demonstrated that even when others try to subvert the message, believers must stay true to the original teachings of Christ, knowing that only the pure Gospel has the power to save. Paul's life and his defense against these distortions call every Christian to hold fast to the truth, to reject any alteration, and to trust that the grace of Jesus is all-sufficient for salvation, needing nothing added and nothing taken away. His unwavering commitment to the true Gospel reminds us that the message of Jesus Christ must remain pure and unchanged, for it is the power of God to everyone who believes, and it must be protected from any form of subversion.

Chapter 19 - Spiritual Warfare

Paul's life as a follower of Christ was filled with constant challenges, both within and without, as he faced an unending battle known as spiritual warfare, a struggle that went beyond the physical world and into realms unseen. In Ephesians 6:12, Paul described this battle by saying, "For we wrestle not against flesh and blood, but against principalities, against powers, against the rulers of the darkness of this world, against spiritual wickedness in high places." These words capture the heart of Paul's experiences, for he knew that his mission to spread the Gospel was not only opposed by people but by dark spiritual forces that sought to hinder God's work at every turn. Throughout his ministry, Paul faced both inner struggles—battling doubts, fears, and the limitations of his own human frailty—and external attacks, such as persecution, imprisonment, and physical harm, all of which were attempts by the enemy to discourage him or stop him entirely. The reality of spiritual warfare was a daily reminder to Paul that his life was a battlefield where he would have to stand strong against forces far beyond human opposition. This warfare wasn't limited to the direct threats he faced from those who opposed his teachings but was a deeper, unseen struggle that affected every part of his journey. Paul's understanding of spiritual warfare helped him recognize that each trial, every plot against him, and all the mockery or slander he encountered were not merely human reactions to his message but were part of a larger, more intense fight orchestrated by spiritual forces opposed to the truth of Christ. These forces, referred to as "principalities" and "powers," represented the organized and deliberate resistance by the kingdom of darkness, aimed at stopping the spread of the light of the Gospel. Paul's battles were often fierce, and they wore on his spirit, for he felt the weight of this warfare in every city he entered, knowing that Satan sought to use discouragement, temptation, and fear to break his resolve. Yet, in the midst of these struggles, Paul found strength not in his own ability but in the armor of God, which he wrote about in

Ephesians 6:13-18, advising believers to "put on the whole armour of God." He understood that the only way to stand firm against these unseen forces was to be spiritually equipped with truth, righteousness, faith, salvation, and the Word of God. Paul himself relied on these pieces of armor, using prayer and Scripture as his defense against the enemy's attacks. His life was a powerful example of resilience, as he faced each day knowing that he was part of a battle that required constant vigilance, prayer, and dependence on God's strength. Paul's writings often reflected his awareness of this spiritual warfare, urging other believers to be aware of the enemy's schemes and to stand firm in their faith, for he knew that every Christian would face similar battles. He encouraged them to persevere, reminding them that victory over these dark forces was possible through Christ, who had already triumphed over sin and death. Paul's experiences showed that spiritual warfare was not a sign of failure or weakness but was evidence of one's commitment to Christ, for the enemy only attacks those who threaten his kingdom. Paul accepted this reality as part of his calling, recognizing that every struggle, whether physical, emotional, or spiritual, was an opportunity to rely more deeply on God. His perspective turned each hardship into a moment of growth, where his faith was tested and refined. Even when he felt weak, Paul would remind himself that God's grace was sufficient, and that God's strength was made perfect in weakness. This truth empowered him to face spiritual warfare with courage, knowing that the battles he fought were not in vain. Paul's journey teaches believers that spiritual warfare is an inevitable part of the Christian life, but one that can be faced with confidence when rooted in God's power. His life reminds us that we are not alone in our struggles, for God equips us with everything we need to withstand the enemy's attacks. Paul's unwavering faith in the face of spiritual warfare encourages us to stand firm, to be vigilant, and to trust that, though the battle may be fierce, victory is assured through Christ. His example calls us to live with purpose and resilience, knowing that every struggle, whether seen or unseen, is part of a larger story where God ultimately triumphs over darkness.

Chapter 20 - Sin of Others

Paul's ministry was filled with many challenges, but one of the most difficult obstacles he faced was the sin of others, especially when disputes and immorality among believers threatened the unity and strength of the early church. His heart was heavy with concern for the spiritual health and purity of the congregations he had founded, and he felt a deep responsibility to address the issues that arose among them. In 1 Corinthians 5:1-2, Paul confronted one of the most troubling cases he encountered, saying, "It is reported commonly that there is fornication among you, and such fornication as is not so much as named among the Gentiles, that one should have his father's wife. And ye are puffed up, and have not rather mourned, that he that hath done this deed might be taken away from among you." Paul was disturbed by the fact that this sin was openly known and yet tolerated within the church, which showed a lack of remorse and a misunderstanding of holiness among the believers. This situation in Corinth was not isolated; Paul dealt with similar issues in other churches, where conflicts, jealousy, pride, and immorality disrupted fellowship and weakened the church's witness to the surrounding communities. As the body of Christ, Paul knew that the church was meant to reflect Jesus's love, purity, and truth, but these sins brought shame and division instead. When believers allowed sin to flourish unchecked, it damaged relationships within the church, causing factions and bitterness to grow. Disputes among believers over issues like favoritism, doctrinal disagreements, and even lawsuits brought before unbelievers, as Paul addressed later in 1 Corinthians 6, weakened the unity that should have been their strength. These issues grieved Paul because he understood that sin's presence among believers hindered their relationship with God and clouded the message of the Gospel. He urged the church to take sin seriously, teaching them that tolerating sin in their midst made it harder for them to stand as a beacon of light to a watching world. Paul's letters often included instructions on how to address these issues, emphasizing the need for repentance, forgiveness, and restoration. He advised church members to lovingly correct one another, not out of judgment but to protect the integrity of their faith. Paul recognized that the sin of others could be like a "little leaven" that leavens the whole lump, spreading through the community and drawing more people into error or complacency. His approach was firm but compassionate, as he wanted the church to understand that true unity could only be achieved by living in alignment with God's standards. Paul's concern for the church's purity was driven by his love for the believers and his desire for them to experience the fullness of God's blessings. He encouraged them to bear one another's burdens, to pray for each other, and to pursue peace, knowing that unity in the Spirit was essential for the church to grow and thrive. Paul also reminded them that they were "ambassadors for Christ" (2 Corinthians 5:20), representing Jesus to the world, and that their behavior should reflect the transformation that came through faith. The presence of disputes, immorality, and pride among the believers saddened Paul because he knew that such issues hindered their spiritual growth and fellowship with God. His letters were filled with pleas for reconciliation, humility, and holiness, as he called the church to rise above their struggles and walk in love, patience, and unity. Paul's efforts to address these issues were not merely to maintain order but to ensure that the church remained a place of healing, truth, and spiritual growth. He warned them that allowing sin to remain unchecked could harden their hearts, weaken their faith, and damage their testimony to others. Paul's guidance on handling the sin of others teaches us that, while conflict and sin may arise within any community, the church is called to a higher standard of grace, humility, and forgiveness. His example reminds us that addressing sin is not about harsh judgment but about protecting the heart and unity of the church, ensuring that it remains a true reflection of Christ's love. Paul's dedication to fostering purity within the church is a powerful reminder that every believer plays a role in maintaining the health of the community, and that by addressing disputes and immorality with compassion and truth, the church can overcome division and stand united in its mission to share the Gospel. Through Paul's letters, we see that the church's unity is not only a gift but a responsibility, one that requires a commitment to love, forgiveness, and the pursuit of holiness for the glory of God.

Chapter 21 - Secret Betrayal

Paul's life as a dedicated servant of Christ was marked by many trials, and one of the most painful experiences he faced was the betrayal and abandonment by those he considered close companions, people he trusted and worked alongside in the mission to spread the Gospel. In 2 Timothy 4:10, Paul expresses this sorrow deeply, saying, "For Demas hath forsaken me, having loved this present world, and is departed unto Thessalonica." Demas had once been a fellow worker, someone who walked beside Paul, sharing in the hardships and joys of ministry, enduring the struggles and rejoicing in the victories. Together, they had likely faced persecution, traveled to new cities, and brought countless people the message of salvation. Yet, despite their shared mission, Demas ultimately chose to leave, drawn away by the lure of the world. This abandonment hurt Paul deeply, not only because he had lost a fellow worker but because it revealed the heartbreaking reality that even those closest to him could turn away. Betrayal by a friend stings in a way that outside opposition never could; it reaches into the heart, creating wounds that take longer to heal. Paul's sadness over Demas's departure was more than personal disappointment; it was a reminder of the spiritual struggle each believer faces between staying true to God's calling and giving in to worldly desires. This wasn't the first or only time Paul had felt the sting of betrayal or abandonment. Throughout his ministry, he encountered people who had once been enthusiastic about the Gospel but later drifted away, either from fear, love of the world, or because they could no longer handle the hardships that came with the mission. Some were likely discouraged by the dangers of persecution, while others may have found the sacrifices too great. Paul's letters reveal that he often felt the weight of this loss, especially during times of imprisonment or intense persecution, when he would have greatly valued the comfort and support of those who understood his mission. Secret betrayal was a painful reality, as people he trusted to stand firm in the faith sometimes let him down. While some, like Timothy and Luke, remained loyal and steadfast, others chose different paths, prioritizing their own safety or desires over the shared calling. Paul's experience with betrayal was a reminder to him—and to all believers—that human relationships, while precious, can sometimes falter under pressure. His sorrow over Demas, and others like him, taught Paul to lean on God even more, realizing that people, however well-meaning, are fallible and sometimes weak. The pain of betrayal, however, did not harden Paul's heart; rather, it deepened his compassion for those who struggled with faith, and it fueled his prayers for strength and perseverance among believers. Paul's experience shows that serving Christ doesn't exempt one from heartbreak or disappointment; in fact, the closer one gets to fulfilling God's work, the more likely they are to encounter such trials. Yet, instead of becoming bitter or disillusioned, Paul chose to continue in his calling, trusting that God understood his heartache and would provide comfort and strength. He poured out his pain in his letters, not to accuse or shame those who left, but to highlight the importance of steadfastness in a world full of distractions and challenges. Paul's endurance despite betrayal serves as an encouragement to believers who might face similar disappointments, teaching them that even when people fail, God's presence is constant. His story reminds us that loyalty to God's mission sometimes requires walking alone, but that such solitude can strengthen one's faith and reliance on the Lord. Paul's response to betrayal was not to give up or grow resentful, but to pray for those who left and to keep moving forward, knowing that his work was for God alone. His experience with Demas is a reminder that true faithfulness is tested in difficult times, and while betrayal may bring sorrow, it also deepens the resolve to stay committed to Christ's calling. Paul's story encourages believers to forgive, to let go of bitterness, and to trust that even when people disappoint, God remains faithful, walking with us through every heartache, strengthening us to complete the journey He has set before us.

Chapter 22 - Satanic Temptations

Paul's life as a servant of Christ was filled with countless trials, and one of the most difficult battles he faced was the constant assault of satanic temptations that sought to discourage him and draw him away from his mission. In 1 Thessalonians 3:5, Paul expresses his concern about the power of temptation when he says, "For this cause, when I could no longer forbear, I sent to know your faith, lest by some means the tempter have tempted you, and our labor be in vain." This verse shows Paul's deep awareness of the enemy's desire to weaken believers' faith, not only among those he had taught but also within himself. He knew that Satan's goal was to discourage, deceive, and deter anyone truly dedicated to spreading the Gospel, using subtle doubts, fears, and hardships as tools to tempt him into giving up. Satanic temptations, for Paul, came in many forms: the physical pain of beatings and imprisonments, the loneliness of being misunderstood or abandoned by others, and the ongoing sense of inadequacy or fear that could arise from facing continual obstacles. These temptations were aimed at making him question his calling, his effectiveness, and even the worthiness of his mission. Paul was aware that such temptations didn't always come as obvious attacks but often came quietly, through moments of fatigue or isolation, trying to plant seeds of discouragement or despair. He knew that the devil's schemes were calculated, meant to wear him down over time, and he was constantly vigilant against these spiritual attacks. Despite his strong faith, Paul still experienced the pull of these temptations, which is why he urged others to remain steadfast and vigilant as well. He recognized that discouragement could slip in when results weren't immediate, when people he trusted turned away, or when he felt physically weak. Satan's goal was to make him feel that the labor, the struggles, and the sacrifices were all in vain. Paul, however, didn't let these temptations defeat him; he combated them with prayer, Scripture, and a relentless focus on God's promises. He reminded himself, and those he wrote to, that they were not alone in these struggles, and that Christ had already overcome the enemy. His letters often reflected his battle against discouragement, but they also radiated hope, as Paul found strength in remembering that his work had eternal value. His determination to continue, despite temptations to quit, showed a depth of faith that inspired the early church and demonstrated that victory over temptation was possible through God's power. Paul's resilience, even when Satan tried to cloud his mind with doubts, serves as a powerful reminder to all believers that spiritual warfare is real, but God equips His people to stand strong. Through every temptation, Paul held on to the knowledge that God was faithful, that his labor was not in vain, and that even the fiercest temptations could not separate him from the love and purpose of Christ. His life encourages us to press on, to resist the voice of discouragement, and to trust that, with God's help, we can overcome every temptation that seeks to hinder our walk of faith.

Chapter 23 – Shackles

Paul's life and mission as a dedicated servant of Christ were filled with countless hardships, but one of the most challenging trials he faced was the constant threat and reality of shackles—imprisonment that restrained his mobility, limited his freedom, and kept him from traveling freely to visit the churches and people he longed to encourage. In Ephesians 3:1, Paul writes, "For this cause I Paul, the prisoner of Jesus Christ for you Gentiles," revealing how he saw himself as a prisoner not merely of Rome or earthly powers but ultimately of Christ, willingly bound for the sake of spreading the Gospel. Though physical chains restricted his movements and forced him into confinement, Paul's spirit remained unbound, and his determination to fulfill God's calling was undeterred by the walls that surrounded him. Imprisonment was a painful reality that Paul faced multiple times throughout his ministry; from Jerusalem to Caesarea, and finally to Rome, he found himself repeatedly placed under guard, his freedom taken from him because of his unwavering commitment to preach about Jesus Christ. For many, such confinement would have brought despair, but Paul chose to see his shackles not as a hindrance but as a unique opportunity to witness to those who guarded him, to fellow prisoners, and to any visitors who came. Rather than letting his imprisonment silence him, Paul turned each prison cell into a place of ministry, continuing to write letters, pray for the churches, and offer encouragement from a distance. Through his letters, now known as the "prison epistles," including Ephesians, Philippians, Colossians, and Philemon, Paul reached out to strengthen believers across regions he could not physically visit. Shackles that should have silenced him became the means by which the message of Christ spread even further, as he penned words that have since inspired countless generations. Paul's response to imprisonment demonstrated his deep faith and trust that God's work could not be stopped by human chains or prison walls. He understood that while his body might be confined, the Word of God was never restricted, and he took comfort in knowing that his suffering could strengthen and encourage others to remain faithful even in difficult times. These shackles, painful and unjust, did not limit the power of the Gospel; instead, they highlighted the resilience of Paul's faith, showing believers that true freedom is found in Christ alone. Paul's imprisonment also served as a powerful testimony to both his fellow Christians and his captors, revealing a man who found purpose even in the darkest circumstances, a man whose hope and joy were unshaken by physical chains. His letters from prison continue to remind believers that no earthly restraint can separate them from God's love or diminish their ability to make an impact for His kingdom. Through Paul's experience with shackles, we learn that challenges and limitations, while difficult, can serve to deepen our faith and extend our reach, for God's power is made perfect in weakness. His life teaches us that even in chains, the Gospel cannot be contained, and that God can use every circumstance, even imprisonment, to spread His truth and inspire others. Paul's unbreakable spirit in the face of confinement encourages us to trust God's purpose in every trial, to believe that He can turn every setback into an opportunity, and to hold on to the hope that, no matter the restraints we face, our lives can still be used for His glory. His legacy as a prisoner of Christ reminds us that true freedom lies not in physical movement but in being bound to the will of God, who can work through us no matter where we are or what limits we face.

Chapter 24 – Sorrow

Paul's life as a servant of Christ was filled with trials and challenges, and one of the deepest burdens he carried was the constant sorrow and concern for the many churches he had helped to establish and strengthen. His heart was continually filled with care for these communities of believers, and the weight of his responsibility to guide, encourage, and protect them often pressed heavily upon him. In 2 Corinthians 11:28, Paul expresses this ongoing burden, saying, "Beside those things that are without, that which cometh upon me daily, the care of all the churches." This statement reveals the depth of Paul's love and commitment to the body of Christ, for he did not merely preach and move on; rather, he carried each church in his heart, feeling their struggles as his own. The people in these churches were like family to him, and their spiritual wellbeing was his constant concern. Paul understood that these young churches were vulnerable, often surrounded by cultures that opposed the message of Christ and faced pressures that could lead them astray. His sorrow came from knowing that false teachings, internal conflicts, persecution, and moral failures threatened the unity and purity of each congregation, and he felt a personal responsibility to help them stay faithful. Although Paul was often separated from them by great distances, his thoughts and prayers remained with them. He would hear reports of disputes, immorality, or confusion creeping into the church, and it pained him deeply, knowing that these issues could harm their faith and witness. Paul's letters, full of both instruction and encouragement, were often written with a heart heavy with sorrow, as he sought to guide these believers back to the truth and strengthen their commitment to Christ. His sorrow wasn't a sign of weakness but of his great love and dedication, showing that he cared not only for their salvation but for their growth and unity as the body of Christ. This burden wasn't something he could easily set aside; it was a daily weight on his heart, and he felt it deeply, especially during times when he himself was facing hardships.

When he was imprisoned or persecuted, he often thought not of his own suffering but of how these churches were faring, hoping they would remain strong and united. Paul's sorrow was mingled with hope, as he trusted that God would protect and sustain them, yet he also knew that each church faced real dangers that could lead them away from the Gospel. His letters, such as those to the Corinthians, Galatians, and Ephesians, reveal his constant desire for these believers to grow in faith, to resist temptation, and to love one another. He urged them to be vigilant, to hold on to the truth, and to walk in the Spirit, knowing that unity and faithfulness were essential for their survival and witness. Paul's sorrow was a reflection of his pastoral heart, a heart that grieved not for himself but for others, desiring above all that they would live lives worthy of the calling they had received in Christ. His experience reminds us that true leadership in the church often involves bearing the weight of others' struggles and standing in the gap for them in prayer. Paul's sorrow teaches us that love for God's people sometimes means sharing in their burdens, feeling their pains, and being willing to sacrifice for their spiritual health. His life shows that caring for the church is not just about teaching or preaching but about bearing a genuine concern for the wellbeing of each believer, and this often involves heartache and sacrifice. Paul's unwavering dedication to the churches he served is a model for all who seek to serve Christ, reminding us that the work of the Gospel is deeply personal and sometimes filled with sorrow, yet it is a sorrow borne out of love and hope. His commitment to nurturing and protecting the faith of others calls us to embrace a similar care for those around us, to pray for them, encourage them, and be willing to carry their burdens as part of our own journey in faith. Through Paul's example, we see that sorrow for the church can be a holy burden, one that draws us closer to God as we intercede for His people and commit to supporting them in love, no matter the cost.

Chapter 25 – Suffering

Paul's life as a faithful servant of Christ was marked by intense suffering and numerous hardships that tested his dedication and endurance every step of the way, yet he pressed on, believing that no hardship was too great if it meant advancing the message of salvation. In 2 Corinthians 11:23-27, Paul gives a glimpse of the trials he faced, saying, "in labours more abundant, in stripes above measure, in prisons more frequent, in deaths oft. Of the Jews five times received I forty stripes save one. Thrice was I beaten with rods, once was I stoned, thrice I suffered shipwreck, a night and a day I have been in the deep; in journeyings often, in perils of waters, in perils of robbers, in perils by mine own countrymen, in perils by the heathen, in perils in the city, in perils in the wilderness, in perils in the sea, in perils among false brethren; in weariness and painfulness, in watchings often, in hunger and thirst, in fastings often, in cold and nakedness." These words paint a vivid picture of the extraordinary sufferings that Paul endured for the sake of the Gospel, and they reveal just how much he sacrificed to fulfill God's calling on his life. Paul's journey was filled with moments that could have easily discouraged or defeated him, but he chose to see each hardship as a part of his mission, a cost he was willing to pay because of his love for Christ and for those he sought to reach with the truth. The beatings, imprisonments, shipwrecks, and constant dangers were more than just physical trials; they were tests of his faith, his resilience, and his trust in God. Each new hardship added to the weight he bore, yet it also strengthened his resolve, teaching him to rely on God's strength rather than his own. Paul's suffering was not only a personal struggle but a testimony to those around him, both believers and unbelievers, who saw a man willing to endure the worst trials without losing his faith or his joy. His willingness to suffer for Christ was a powerful example, showing the early church that following Jesus might mean enduring pain and loss, yet that these sacrifices were worth it for the eternal reward that awaited. Every beating, every cold night, and every moment of hunger was a reminder of Paul's commitment to his calling, for he did not see his suffering as a reason to quit but as proof of his dedication to the Gospel. He knew that his hardships were temporary, that they were "light affliction" compared to the eternal glory that would one day be revealed, as he wrote in 2 Corinthians 4:17. Paul's suffering also served to draw him closer to Christ, who had Himself suffered greatly, and he saw his trials as a way to share in the sufferings of his Savior. This perspective transformed his pain into something meaningful, giving him the strength to endure and to encourage others who faced similar struggles. Paul's hardships were not in vain; through his suffering, he reached countless people, planted churches, and inspired believers to stay faithful no matter the cost. His letters, written from prison cells and places of great distress, carry messages of hope, joy, and perseverance, showing that even in suffering, God's grace is sufficient. Paul's life reminds us that the path of faith is often difficult, filled with trials that test our commitment, but that God is with us in every hardship, providing strength and purpose. His example teaches us that suffering for Christ is not something to fear but to embrace as part of the journey, for it refines our character, deepens our faith, and draws us closer to God. Paul's willingness to endure general hardships, even to the point of death, challenges us to examine our own commitment to Christ and to find strength in knowing that every trial we face has meaning and purpose in God's plan. Through Paul's life, we see that suffering is not a sign of defeat but of faithfulness, a testimony to the world that the Gospel is worth any cost. His story encourages believers to remain steadfast, to trust in God's sustaining power, and to remember that in every hardship, Christ walks with us, turning our suffering into a powerful witness for His glory. Paul's legacy of endurance in the face of suffering is a lasting reminder that no hardship can separate us from the love of God, and that even the greatest trials can be used for His glory, shaping us into vessels of His grace and truth.

Conclusion

In I Thessalonians 2:18, Paul's words, "Wherefore we would have come unto you, even I Paul, once and again; but Satan hindered us," remind us of the persistent challenges he faced on his mission to spread the Gospel and build up the early church. This verse highlights the central theme of "Held Back, But Not Defeated", revealing the incredible perseverance and faith that defined Paul's journey. Throughout the book, we've examined Paul's experiences of being hindered, held back, and opposed by forces far beyond his control—imprisonments, beatings, betrayals, and even spiritual attacks. Yet, each time Paul encountered an obstacle, he chose not to see it as a reason to give up but as a call to lean deeper into his faith in God. Paul knew that his hardships were not pointless; instead, they became opportunities for God to work through him in unexpected ways. He wrote letters from prison that strengthened believers, he shared the Gospel with guards and officials who would have never heard it otherwise, and he showed countless Christians that obstacles do not equate to defeat. As modern believers reflect on Paul's example, they find a powerful message for their own lives: while the Christian path may be filled with struggles, these trials do not signify failure. Paul's story teaches us that even when we face discouragement, opposition, or times when it feels like our efforts are blocked, we are never truly defeated if we keep our trust in God. The same God who helped Paul overcome so much stands with believers today, offering the strength and grace to face their own challenges. The book's conclusion underscores that the trials faced by Paul are not unlike those Christians encounter now, whether in struggles against temptation, moments of doubt, or times when life's circumstances seem overwhelming. By holding onto faith and continuing forward, Christians today can experience the same kind of victories Paul did—victories that reveal God's power and bring hope to others. "Held Back, But Not Defeated" is a call to press on, to keep faith even when things seem uncertain, and to trust that God's purpose will be fulfilled, just as it was in Paul's life. Through Paul's triumphs in the face of trials, Christians are encouraged to find strength in their relationship with Christ, knowing that every hardship, like those Paul endured, can be turned into a testament of God's faithfulness. The journey of faith is rarely easy, but with Paul's story as an example, we are reminded that nothing—neither setbacks nor hardships—can separate us from the love and victory we have in Jesus. In this, believers find courage to continue their own journey, assured that, like Paul, they may be held back at times, but they are never defeated.

Don't miss out!

Visit the website below and you can sign up to receive emails whenever Joshua Rhoades publishes a new book. There's no charge and no obligation.

https://books2read.com/r/B-A-AJLBB-QWDHF

BOOKS 2 READ

Connecting independent readers to independent writers.

Did you love *Held Back But Not Defeated*? Then you should read *Renewed Hope- How to Find Encouragement in God*[1] by Joshua Rhoades!

[2]

In a world where challenges and hardships seem to come at us from every side, it's easy to feel overwhelmed, discouraged, and even hopeless. We all face moments when we wonder how we will ever make it through the difficulties we encounter. But in these times, the Bible offers us a powerful example of finding strength and hope, no matter the circumstances. In 1 Samuel 30:6, we read about David, a man who faced great trials and overwhelming odds, yet in the midst of it all, "David encouraged himself in the LORD his God." This simple yet profound statement serves as the foundation for this book, "Renewed Hope- How to Find Encouragement in God." David's life was filled with ups and downs, moments of triumph and times of deep despair. He knew what it was like to be pursued by enemies, to experience loss, and to feel abandoned. Yet, even in his darkest hours, David found a way to renew his hope by turning to God. He didn't rely on his own strength or seek comfort in worldly solutions. Instead, he looked to the LORD, drawing strength and encouragement from his relationship with God. This book is an invitation to explore how we, too, can find renewed hope and encouragement in God, just as David did. It is a guide to understanding the power of faith, prayer, and trusting in God's promises, even when life seems unbearable. Throughout these pages, we will explore practical ways to draw closer to God, to encourage ourselves in Him, and to discover the peace and strength

1. https://books2read.com/u/boeko1
2. https://books2read.com/u/boeko1

that come from relying on the LORD. Whether you are facing a specific challenge right now or simply want to deepen your relationship with God, this book will provide you with the tools and inspiration you need to find encouragement in the LORD. As we journey together through the principles found in David's example, you will learn how to shift your focus from the problems that surround you to the God who sustains you. You will discover that no matter what life throws at you, there is always hope in the LORD, and by encouraging yourself in Him, you can face any situation with renewed strength and confidence. This is not just a book about surviving difficult times, but about thriving through them by finding your hope and encouragement in the unchanging character of God. So, whether you are struggling with personal challenges, feeling weighed down by the burdens of life, or simply seeking a deeper sense of peace and purpose, "Renewed Hope- How to Find Encouragement in God" is here to remind you that you are not alone, and that with God, there is always a reason to hope. Let David's example inspire you to turn to the LORD, to find your strength in Him, and to walk forward with a renewed sense of hope, no matter what you face.

www.ingramcontent.com/pod-product-compliance
Lightning Source LLC
LaVergne TN
LVHW091227150826
845673LV00003B/1051
9798227332387